FOREWO

Some years ago, a researcher decided to find the secret of success. After months of study and countless interviews, he finally gave up. "There is not a secret," he said, "it is all related to hard work. One must climb the ladder to success, not just be lifted on an elevator."

The successful individual is the one who will do what the average person will not do. And average is nothing more than being the top of the bottom.

Thinking wrong, believing wrong, and confessing wrong always leads to an unhappy, mediocre and unprofitable way of life.

To think success, to become better, to believe big and to strive to be above average, you must develop the right kind of mental processes.

You have been programmed to be negative, to disbelieve, to be skeptical. However, you can change. That negative experience, the minuses — these can be transformed into positives and pluses simply by changing your attitudes.

William James said, "The greatest discovery of my generation is that men can change their circumstances by changing their attitude of mind."

We teach changing those thoughts by changing the input. What goes in must come out. You control the future because you have the power to control your thoughts.

Some say success is just a decision away. That is true, on the surface. But that decision must be backed up with solid effort.

A person with a winning attitude accounts for 80 percent of the results in this country today. It's amazing that the figures don't change from year to year. They stay about the same. Twenty percent of the people are getting 80 percent of the results and 80 percent of the people are getting 20 percent of the results. That isn't very much when you realize these figures haven't changed over the last 25 years.

Your growth potential, return on your investment, rewards in proportion to your efforts, and personal independence are limited only by your vision and desire. This already has made you above average.

So be enthusiastic! You have a lot to be excited about. God created you in the likeness of Himself and endowed you with specific talents and abilities. As you develop those areas in your life and use them to help others, you won't have to be concerned about being above average. You will have conquered that enemy.

Dexter R. Yager Sr.

"John, you have really hit the target with your excellent book, *An Enemy Called Average*. Mediocrity continues to plague business, ministry, and personal performance. Your book, with its bite-sized nuggets, helps break this cycle and helps provide positive direction and insight to any organization or individual. Congratulations on a really outstanding book!"

Van Crouch, Author/President,
Van Crouch Communications

• • •

"It is a simple but profound book. A practical book that people need to read and be doers of."

John L. Meares, Bishop, Evangel Temple
Washington, D.C.

• • •

"I've read it on my travels and thoroughly enjoy what you're saying. I've ordered copies of your book and am sending a copy to each of our supporting ministers as a gift from me. Truly the Lord has given you the 'pen of a ready writer.' "

Dick Mills, Author/Minister

• • •

"I found it to be thought-provoking, impressive, and inspirational. We are with you in your war against mediocrity."

Morris Cerullo, President,
Morris Cerullo Ministries/Inspirational Network

• • •

"Thanks for encouraging us all to be the best we can be for Christ."

Tony Campolo, Author/Instructor

"I believe it will be helpful to many of God's people."
B. J. Wilhite, President, National Prayer Embassy

• • •

"An Enemy Called Average, an excellent title."
Charles Stanley, Pastor, The First Baptist Church
Atlanta, Georgia

• • •

"I believe the release of this book is timely and will be effective in calling the Body of Christ to excellence."
Earl Paulk, D.D., Bishop,
Chapel Hill Harvester Church
Decatur, Georgia

• • •

"I did find in your book several compilations I want to keep for future reference."
Donald K. Campbell,
President, Dallas Theological Seminary

• • •

"I'm so impressed that I'm quoting it in our new tabloid."
Charles and Francis Hunter, Authors/Ministers

• • •

"I've used it in some of my 'Wisdom for Achievers' services. Please write another one."
Dr. Coy Barker, Senior Pastor, Faith Tabernacle
Oklahoma City, Oklahoma

• • •

"I want to encourage you to keep producing books of this sort. They are greatly needed to motivate believers to a more effective and dynamic Christian lifestyle."
Robert Walker, President of Christian Life Missions

AN ENEMY
CALLED AVERAGE

by
John L. Mason

14th Printing
Over 185,000 Copies in Print

An Enemy Called Average
ISBN 0-89274-765-X
Copyright © 1990 by John Mason
P. O. Box 54996
Tulsa, OK 74155

CONTENTS

Part III: Looking Upward

DEDICATION

I am proud to dedicate this book to my beautiful wife, Linda, and our four wonderful children, Michelle, Greg, Mike, and David.

To Linda, for her steadfastness and love;

To Michelle, for her creativity and enthusiasm;

To Greg, for his patient perseverance and willingness to help;

To Mike, who through his little boy love for me reminds me how we are to love the Father.

To David, who, as an infant, always keeps my perspective accurate.

Without their support, help, encouragement, sense of humor, and prayers, this book would still be sitting in the various and sundry files from whence it came.

ACKNOWLEDGMENTS

It is impossible to write a book like this one without the help of "foundational-level" people. Special thanks to:

My pastor, Billy Joe Daugherty, whose messages have consistently inspired me to bound past mediocrity;

Roberts Liardon, who challenged me to walk in the Spirit and not live another day in neutral;

Keith Provance, the best example of a leader I have ever known;

Mike Loomis, who always offers a timely word of encouragement.

Tim Redmond, whose insight and advice has been invaluable.

INTRODUCTION

Mediocrity is a region bounded on the north by compromise, on the south by indecision, on the east by past thinking, and on the west by a lack of vision.

One morning as I woke up, the first thought that came to my mind before my feet hit the floor was the phrase "An Enemy Called Average." At that moment I knew that God had given me the title for the book which had been stirring within me for so long.

The purpose of this book is to address areas in your life that need improvement and to stir up the God-given gifts and call within you. Every person has been endowed with a certain mixture of abilities and opportunities which makes him unique. No mixture is insignificant. There is something that God has placed within each of us that causes us to cry out to be above average and extraordinary.

I felt led to write this book in a "nugget" style in order to deliver as much meat as possible in an enjoyable, easy-to-read format. Since there are 52 nuggets, this book can be used as an excellent once-a-week devotional or for personal development.

In Genesis, chapter three, verse nine, God asked Adam, "Where are you?" He is still asking that question of each of us today. Where are we in regard to God's plan for our lives? Where are we concerning the gifts and talents He has given us?

It is my prayer that as you read this book, you will allow the Holy Spirit to reveal God's plan for you and to inform, exhort, and correct you so that you will bound past every area of mediocrity and find total fulfillment in your life.

PART I:
LOOKING INWARD

YOUR LEAST FAVORITE COLOR SHOULD BE BEIGE.

Never try to defend your present position and situation. Choose to be a person who is on the offensive, not the defensive. **People who live defensively never rise above being average.** We're called, as Christians, to be on the offensive, to take the initiative. A lukewarm, indecisive person is never secure regardless of his wealth, education, or position.

Don't ever let your quest for balance become an excuse for not taking the unique, radical, invading move that God has directed you to take. Many times the attempt to maintain balance in life is really just an excuse for being lukewarm. In Joshua 1:6,7,9 the Lord says three times to Joshua, "Be strong and courageous." I believe that He is saying the same thing to all believers today.

When you choose to be on the offensive, the atmosphere of your life will begin to change. So if you don't like the atmosphere of your life, choose to take the offensive position. Taking the offensive is not just an action taken outside a person; it is always a decision made within.

When you do choose to be on the offensive, keep all your conflicts impersonal. Fight the issue, not the person. Speak about what God in you can do, not what others cannot do. **You will find that when all of your reasons are defensive, your cause almost never succeeds.**

Being on the offensive and taking the initiative is a master key which opens the door to opportunity in your life. Learn to create a habit of taking the initiative and **don't ever start your day in neutral.** Every morning when your feet hit the floor, you should be thinking on the offensive, reacting like an invader, taking control of your day and your life.

By pulling back and being defensive usually you enhance the problem. Intimidation always precedes defeat. If you are not sure which way to go, pray and move towards the situation in confident trust.

Be like the two fishermen who got trapped in a storm in the middle of the lake. One turned to the other and asked, "Should we pray, or should we row?" His wise companion responded, "Let's do both!"

That's taking the offensive.

GROWTH COMES FROM BUILDING ON TALENTS, GIFTS, AND STRENGTHS — NOT BY SOLVING PROBLEMS.

One of the most neglected areas in many people's lives is the area of gifts that God has placed within them. It is amazing how some people can devote their entire lives to a field of endeavor or a profession that has nothing to do with their inborn talents. In fact, the opposite is also true. Many people spend their whole lifetime trying to change who God has made them. They ignore their God-given blessings while continually seeking to change their natural makeup. As children of God, we need to recognize our innate gifts, talents, and strengths and do everything in our power to build on them.

One good thing about God's gifts and calling is that they are permanent and enduring. Romans 11:29 tells us: *...the gifts and calling of God are without repentance.* The Greek word translated *repentance* in this verse means "irrevocable." God cannot take away His gifts and calling in your life. **Even if you've never done anything with them, even if you've failed time and time again, God's gifts and calling are still resident within you.** They are there this day, and you can choose to do something with them, beginning right now.

Gifts and talents are really God's deposits in our personal accounts, but we determine the interest on them. The greater the amount of interest and attention we give to them, the greater their value becomes. **God's gifts are never loans; they are always deposits.** As such, they are never used up or depleted. In fact, the more they are used, the greater, stronger, and more valuable they become. When they are put to good use, they provide information, insight, and revelation which cannot be received any other way or from any other source.

As Christians, we need to make full use of all the gifts and talents which God has bestowed upon us so that we do not abound in one area while becoming bankrupt in another. Someone has said, "If the only tool you have is a hammer, you tend to treat everything like a nail." Don't make that mistake; use all of the gifts God has given you. If you choose not to step out and make maximum use of the gifts and talents in your life, you will spend your days on this earth helping someone else reach his goals. Most people let others control their destiny. Don't allow anyone to take over the driver's seat in your life. Fulfill your own dreams and determine your own life's course.

Never underestimate the power of the gifts that are within you. **Gifts and talents are given us to use not only so we can fulfill to the fullest the call in our own lives, but also so we can reach the souls who are attached to those gifts.** There are people whose lives are waiting to be affected by what God has placed within you. So evaluate yourself. Define and refine your gifts, talents and strengths. Choose today to look for opportunities to exercise your unique God-endowed, God-ordained gifts and calling.

"THE NOSE OF THE BULLDOG IS SLANTED BACKWARDS SO HE CAN CONTINUE TO BREATHE WITHOUT LETTING GO." — WINSTON CHURCHILL

Persistent people begin their success where most others quit. We Christians need to be known as people of persistence and endurance. **One person with commitment, persistence, and endurance will accomplish more than a thousand people with interest alone.** In Hebrews 12:1 (NIV) we read: *Therefore, since we are surrounded by such a great cloud of witnesses, let us throw off everything that hinders and the sin that so easily entangles, and let us run with perseverance the race marked out for us.* The more diligently we work, the harder it is to quit. Persistence is a habit; so is quitting.

Never worry about how much money, ability, or equipment you are starting with. Just begin with a million dollars worth of determination. Remember: **it's not what you have, it's what you do with what you have that makes all the difference.** Many people eagerly begin "the good fight of faith," but they forget to add patience, persistence, and endurance to their enthusiasm. Josh Billings said: "Consider the postage stamp. Its usefulness consists in the ability to stick to something until it gets there." You and I should be known as "postage-stamp" Christians.

In First Corinthians 15:58, the Apostle Paul writes: *Therefore, my beloved brethren, be ye stodfast,*

19

unmoveable, *always abounding in the work of the Lord, forasmuch as ye know that your labour is not in vain in the Lord.* Peter tells us: *Wherefore, beloved, seeing that ye look for such things, be diligent that ye may be found of him in peace, without spot, and blameless* (2 Pet. 3:14). And wise Solomon points out: *Seest thou a man diligent in his business? he shall stand before kings...*(Prov. 22:29).

In the Far East the people plant a tree called the Chinese bamboo. During the first four years they water and fertilize the plant with seemingly little or no results. Then the fifth year they again apply water and fertilizer — and in five weeks' time the tree grows ninety feet in height! The obvious question is: did the Chinese bamboo tree grow ninety feet in five weeks, or did it grow ninety feet in five years? The answer is: it grew ninety feet in five years. Because if at any time during those five years the people had stopped watering and fertilizing the tree, it would have died.

Many times our dreams and plans appear not to be succeeding. We are tempted to give up and quit trying. Instead, we need to continue to water and fertilize those dreams and plans, nurturing the seeds of the vision God has placed within us. Because we know that if we do not quit, if we display perseverance and endurance, we will also reap a harvest. Charles Haddon Spurgeon said, "By perseverance the snail reached the ark." We need to be like that snail.

WE CAN GROW BY OUR QUESTIONS, AS WELL AS BY OUR ANSWERS.

Here are some important questions we should ask ourselves:

1. What one decision would I make if I knew that it would not fail?
2. What one thing should I eliminate from my life because it holds me back from reaching my full potential?
3. Am I on the path of something absolutely marvelous, or something absolutely mediocre?
4. If everyone in the United States of America were on my level of spirituality, would there be a revival in the land?
5. Does the devil know who I am?
6. Am I running from something, or to something?
7. What can I do to make better use of my time?
8. Would I recognize Jesus if I met Him on the street?
9. Who do I need to forgive?
10. What is my favorite scripture for myself, my family, my career?
11. What impossible thing am I believing and planning for?
12. What is my most prevailing thought?

13. What good thing have I previously committed myself to do that I have quit doing?
14. Of the people I respect most, what is it about them that earns my respect?
15. What would a truly creative person do in my situation?
16. What outside influences are causing me to be better or worse?
17. Can I lead anyone else to Christ?
18. In what areas do I need improvement in terms of personal development?
19. What gifts, talents, or strengths do I have?
20. What is one thing that I can do for someone else who has no opportunity to repay me?

DON'T ASK TIME WHERE IT'S GONE; TELL IT WHERE TO GO.

$\mathcal{A}$ll great achievers, all successful people, are those who have been able to gain control over their time. It has been said that all human beings have been created equal in one respect: each person has been given 24 hours each day.

We need to choose to give our best time to our most challenging situation. It's not how much we do that matters; it's how much we get done. We should choose to watch our time, not our watch. One of the best timesavers is the ability to say no. Not saying no when you should is one of the biggest wastes of time you will ever experience.

Don't spend a dollar's worth of time for ten cent's worth of results.

Make sure to take care of the vulnerable times in your days. These vulnerable times are the first thing in the morning and the last thing at night. I have heard a minister say that what a person is like at midnight when he is all alone reveals that person's true self.

Never allow yourself to say, "I could be doing big things if I weren't so busy doing small things!" Take control of your time. **The greater control you exercise over your time, the greater freedom you will experience**

in your life. The psalmist prayed, *So teach us to number our days, that we may apply our hearts unto wisdom* (Ps. 90:12). The Bible teaches us that the devil comes to steal, and to kill, and to destroy (John 10:10), and this verse applies to time as well as to people. The enemy desires to provide God's children with ideas of how to kill, steal, and destroy valuable time.

People are always saying, "I'd give anything to be able to...." There is a basic leadership principle that says, "6 x 1 = 6." If you want to write a book, learn to play a musical instrument, become a better tennis player, or do anything else important, then you should devote one hour a day, six days a week, to the project. Sooner than you think, what you desire will become reality. There are not many things that a person cannot accomplish in 312 hours a year! Just a commitment of one hour a day, six days a week, is all it takes.

We all have the same amount of time each day. The difference between people is determined by what they do with the amount of time at their disposal. Don't be like the airline pilot flying over the Pacific Ocean who reported to his passengers, "We're lost, but we're making great time!" Remember that the future arrives an hour at a time. **Gain control of your time, and you will gain control of your life.**

NUGGET #6

OBEY THE NINTH COMMANDMENT.

For those of us who are not Bible scholars, the essence of the Ninth Commandment can be summarized in one statement, "Thou shalt not lie." Each Christian should be a person of unquestionable integrity. For us, gray is never right; it must be either black or white.

Hope built on a lie is always the beginning of loss. Never attempt to build anything on a foundation of lies and half-truths. It will not stand.

It has been said that it should be easy to make an honest living because there is so little competition. Actually **only a person with honesty and integrity can be accurately motivated or directed.** Lying will always distort God's guidance in your life. It will cause you to take steps that are not right for you. It will produce greater loss than whatever savings you may gain by telling an untruth.

Lying becomes a very easy habit. The fact is that a person who allows himself to lie once will find it much easier to do so a second time. Lying is also a trap. No one has a good enough memory to be a successful liar. T.L. Osborn says, "Always tell the truth, and you never have to remember what you said."

In Proverbs 12:22 we read, *Lying lips are an abomination to the Lord: but they that deal truly are his delight.* Proverbs 19:9 declares, *A false witness shall not be unpunished, and he that speaketh lies shall perish.* In Colossians 3:9,10 the Apostle Paul admonishes us:

Lie not one to another, seeing that ye have put off the old man with his deeds;

And have put on the new man, which is renewed in knowledge after the image of him that created him.

There are seven results of lying. If you lie:

1. You will attract liars into your life. (Prov. 17:4.)
2. You will have a lack of understanding. (Ps. 119:104.)
3. You will never enjoy permanent results. (Prov. 12:19; 21:28.)
4. You will end up in bondage. (Gal. 2:4.)
5. You will be punished. (Prov. 19:5.)
6. You will become a fool. (Prov. 10:18.)
7. Your lies will come back upon you. (Ps. 7:14-16.)

Little white lies grow up to be big black lies. Decide and determine to be free from the bondage of breaking the Ninth Commandment.

A MAN WITH ONE WATCH KNOWS WHAT TIME IT IS; A MAN WITH TWO IS NEVER QUITE SURE.
— ANONYMOUS QUOTE

Have you ever noticed that some of the most miserable people in the world are those who can never make a decision? **When the human mind is in doubt, it is most easily swayed by the slightest of impulses.** This opens the door to many, many wrong decisions. Many times indecision allows things to go from bad to worse. Indecision is deadly. The truth is that the most dangerous place to be is in the middle of the road.

We believers should be the most decisive of all people. Christian leaders should have wills, not wishes. In James 1:8 the Bible says, *A double minded man is unstable in all his ways.* An indecisive person allows instability to creep into every area of his life. If we don't decide what is important in our own lives, we will probably end up doing only the things that are important to others. **The greater the degree of wishful thinking, the greater the degree of mediocrity.** Being decisive, being focused, committing ourselves to the fulfillment of a dream, greatly increases our probability of success. It also closes the door to wrong options.

The challenge for all of us is to be dedicated dreamers, or perhaps I should say, decisive dreamers. Harry Truman once said, "Some questions cannot be answered, but they can be decided." Most of the time, you and I may not have all the facts available about any given situation, but we will usually have all the facts we need to make a decision. The Bible says to let the peace of God rule in our hearts. (Col. 3:15.) *The Amplified Bible* version tells us to let the peace which comes from Christ act as an umpire in our hearts.

Be decisive. Go with the peace of God and do not be afraid to make a decision. The fact is that decisive people typically prevail and rise to the top because most people are indecisive.

If you are neutral on spiritual matters, you will likely find yourself operating against heaven. Thank God we serve a decisive Lord. He has given us His peace and His Word so we can make wise decisions. We should not be the kind of people who claim that God has told us one thing this week and the very opposite next week. God does not change His degrees that quickly. Nor does He ever direct anyone to act contrary to the good sense and sound judgment shown in His Word.

God desires that we be decisive in our lives. As His children we should be like our heavenly Father, with Whom there is *"no variableness, neither shadow of turning."* (James 1:17.) We should be people of great wills. **If the devil controls our will, he controls our destiny. But if God controls our will, then He controls our destiny.**

The choice is ours. Let's be decisive. Let's make the right decision!

DON'T CONSUME YOUR TOMORROWS FEEDING ON YOUR YESTERDAYS.

Decide today to get rid of any "loser's limps" which you may still be carrying from some past experience. As followers of Jesus Christ, you and I need to break the power of the past to dominate our present and determine our future.

In Luke 9:62, Jesus said, ...*No man, having put his hand to the plough, and looking back, is fit for the kingdom of God.* If we are not careful, we will allow the past to exercise a great hold on us. **The more we look backward, the less able we are to see forward.** The past makes no difference concerning what God can do for us today.

That is the beauty of the Christian life. Even when we have failed, we are able to ask for forgiveness and be totally cleansed of and released from our past actions. Whatever hold the past may have on us can be broken. It is never God Who holds us back. It is always our own choosing to allow the past to keep us from living to the fullest in the present and future. Failure is waiting around the corner for those who are living off of yesterday's successes and failures. **We should choose to be forward-focused, not past-possessed.** We should learn to profit from the past, but to invest in the future.

In Philippians 3:13,14, the Apostle Paul writes:

Brethren, I count not myself to have apprehended: but this one thing I do, forgetting those things which are behind, and reaching forth unto those things which are before,

I press toward the mark for the prize of the high calling of God in Christ Jesus.

The key here is "forgetting those things which are behind" in order to reach for "the high calling of God in Christ Jesus." To fulfill our calling in Christ, we must first forget that which lies behind. Probably the most common stronghold in a person's life is his past mistakes and failures. Today is the day to begin to shake off the shackles of the past and move forward.

The past is past. It has no life.

THE BEST TIME OF DAY IS NOW.

Procrastination is a killer.

When you choose to kill time, you begin to kill those gifts and callings which God has placed within your life. The Living Bible paraphrase of Ecclesiastes 11:4 reads: *If you wait for perfect conditions, you will never get anything done.*

The first step in overcoming procrastination is to eliminate all excuses and reasons for not taking decisive and immediate action.

Everybody is on the move. They are moving forwards, backwards, or on a treadmill. The mistake most people make is thinking that the main goal of life is to stay busy. Such thinking is a trap. What is important is not whether a person is busy, but whether he is progressing. It is a question of activity versus accomplishment.

A gentleman named John Henry Fabre conducted an experiment with processionary caterpillars. They are so named because of their peculiar habit of blindly following each other no matter how they are lined up or where they are going. This man took a group of these tiny creatures and did something interesting with them. He placed them in a circle. For 24 hours the caterpillars dutifully followed one another around and around. Then he did something else. He placed the caterpillars around a saucer full of pine needles (their favorite food). For six days the mindless creatures moved around and around the saucer, literally dying from starvation and exhaustion even though an abundance of choice food was located less than two inches away.

You see, they had confused activity with accomplishment.

We Christians need to be known as those who accomplish great things for God — not those who simply talk about it. Procrastinators are good at talking versus doing. It is true what Mark Twain said: "Noise produces nothing. Often a hen who has merely laid an egg cackles as though she has laid an asteroid."

We need to be like the apostles. They were never known much for their policies or procedures, their theories or excuses. Instead, they were known for their acts. Many people say that they are waiting for God; but in most cases God is waiting for them. We need to say with the psalmist, "Lord, my times are in Your hands." (Ps. 31:15.) The price of growth is always less than the cost of stagnation. As Edmund Burke said, "The only thing necessary for the triumph of evil is for good men to do nothing."

Occasionally you may see someone who doesn't do anything, and yet seems to be successful in life. Don't be deceived. The old saying is true: "Even a broken clock is right twice a day." As Christians we are called to make progress — not excuses.

Procrastination is a primary tool of the devil to hold us back and to make us miss God's timing in our lives. *The desire of the slothful killeth him; for his hands refuse to labour* (Prov. 21:25). **The fact is, the longer we take to act on God's direction, the more unclear it becomes.**

FEAR AND WORRY ARE INTEREST PAID IN ADVANCE ON SOMETHING YOU MAY NEVER OWN.

Fear is a poor chisel to carve out tomorrow. Worry is simply the triumph of fear over faith.

There's a story that is told about a woman who was standing on a street corner crying profusely. A man came up to her and asked why she was weeping. The lady shook her head and replied: "I was just thinking that maybe someday I would get married. We would later have a beautiful baby girl. Then one day this child and I would go for a walk along this street, come to this corner, and my darling daughter would run into the street, get hit by a car, and die."

Now that sounds like a pretty ridiculous situation — for a grown woman to be weeping her eyes out because of something that would probably never happen. Yet isn't this the way we respond when we worry? We take a situation or event which might never exist and build it up all out of proportion in our mind.

There is an old Swedish proverb that says, "Worry gives a small thing a big shadow." **Worry is simply the misuse of God's creative imagination which He has placed within each of us.** When fear rises in our mind, we should learn to expect the opposite in our life.

The word *worry* itself is derived from an Anglo-Saxon term meaning "to strangle," or "to choke off." There is no question that worry and fear in the mind does choke off the creative flow from above.

Things are seldom as they seem. "Skim milk masquerades as cream," said W.S. Gilbert. As we dwell on and worry about matters beyond our control, a negative effect begins to set in. Too much analysis always leads to paralysis. **Worry is a route which leads from somewhere to nowhere. Don't let it direct your life.**

In Psalm 55:22 the Bible says, *Cast thy burden upon the Lord, and he shall sustain thee: he shall never suffer the righteous to be moved.* Never respond out of fear, and never fear to respond. Action attacks fear; inaction builds fear.

Don't worry and don't fear. Instead, take your fear and worry to the Lord, *Casting all your care upon him; for he careth for you* (1 Pet. 5:7).

OUR WORDS ARE SEEDS PLANTED INTO OTHER PEOPLE'S LIVES.

What we say is important. The Bible states that out of the abundance of the heart the mouth speaks. (Matt. 12:34.) We need to change our vocabulary. We need to speak words of life and light. Our talk should always rise to the level of the Word of God.

We Christians should be known as people who speak positively, those who speak the Word of God into situations, those who speak forth words of life.

We should not be like the man who joined a monastery in which the monks were allowed to speak only two words every seven years. After the first seven years had passed, the new initiate met with the abbot who asked him, "Well, what are your two words?"

"Food's bad," replied the man, who then went back to spend another seven-year period before once again meeting with his ecclesiastical superior.

"What are your two words now?" asked the clergyman.

"Bed's hard," responded the man.

Seven years later — twenty-one years after his initial entry into the monastery — the man met with the abbot for the third and final time.

"And what are your two words this time?" he was asked.

"I quit."

"Well, I'm not surprised," answered the disgusted cleric, "all you've done since you got here is complain!"

Don't be like that man; don't be known as a person whose only words are negative.

If you are a member of the "murmuring grapevine," you need to resign. In John 6:43 our Lord instructed His disciples, ...*Murmur not among yourselves*. In Philippians 2:14,15 the Apostle Paul exhorted the believers of his day:

Do all things without murmurings and disputings:

That ye may be blameless and harmless, the sons of God, without rebuke, in the midst of a crooked and perverse nation, among whom ye shine as lights in the world.

Contrary to what you may have heard, talk is not cheap. Talk is very expensive. We should know that our words are powerful. What we say affects what we get from others, and what others get from us. When we speak the wrong word, it lessens our ability to see and hear the will of God.

VERSUS.

Every day we make decisions. Daily we are confronted with options. **We must choose one or the other.** We cannot have both. These options include:

Being bitter versus being better.
Indifference versus decisiveness.
Lukewarmness versus enthusiasm.
"If we can" versus "how we can."
"Give up" versus "get up."
Security versus risk.
Coping with evil versus overcoming evil.
Blending in versus standing out.
How much we do versus how much we get done.
Coexisting with darkness versus opposing darkness.
Destruction versus development.
Resisting versus receiving.
Complaining versus obtaining.
Trying versus committing.
Peace versus strife.
Choice versus chance.
Determination versus discouragement.
Growing versus dying.
Demanding more of ourselves versus excusing ourselves.

Doing for others versus doing for self.
Progress versus regression.
Steering versus drifting.
Priorities versus aimlessness.
Accountability versus irresponsibility.
Action versus activity.
Solutions versus problems.
More of God versus more of everything else.
Being in "Who's Who" versus asking "Why me?"

KEEP YOUR FEET ON THE ROCK WHEN YOU REACH THE END OF YOUR ROPE.

Don't quit. There is a big difference between quitting and changing. I believe that **when God sees someone who doesn't quit, He looks down and says, "There is someone I can use."**

In Galatians 6:9 (NIV) we are told, *Let us not become weary in doing good, for at the proper time we will reap a harvest if we do not give up.* Look at this verse carefully. It urges us not to become weary, assuring us that we will — not might — reap a harvest if we do not give up.

God doesn't quit. It is impossible for Him to do so. In Philippians 1:6 (NIV) the Apostle Paul writes about *being confident of this, that he who began a good work in you will carry it on to completion until the day of Christ Jesus.* There are several important points in this verse. The most crucial is the fact that God does not quit. Therefore, we can have great confidence that He will complete the good work He has begun in us. He will see us through every step of the way until we have reached our ultimate destination.

One of the best scriptural examples of a person who did not quit is Joseph. He had many reasons to justify giving up. First, when he was trapped in the pit into which his brothers had thrown him because of their jealousy, I am sure he said to himself, "This is not the way I dreamed my life would work out." Later on, he had a marvelous opportunity to become discouraged and quit when he was unjustly accused and thrown into prison for a crime he did not commit. Again he could have said to himself, "This is not right; I'm not supposed to be here."

But eventually the dream which God had given Joseph became reality. He was elevated from prisoner to prime minister in one day. Although Joseph did not know or understand the steps through which the Lord would lead him, he remained true to his God. Despite the trials and obstacles he faced, he did not quit.

There is no greater reward than that which comes as a result of holding fast to the Word and will of God. Only you can decide not to lose. Most people quit right on the verge of success. Often it is right at their fingertips. There is only one degree of difference between hot water and steam.

In Luke 18 (NIV) Jesus told the parable of the persistent widow. The Bible reveals His purpose in relating this story: *Then Jesus told his disciples a parable to show them they should always pray and not give up* (v. 1). The psalmist tells us, *Commit thy way unto the Lord; trust also in him; and he shall bring it to pass* (Ps. 37:5).

The only way we can lose is to quit. That is the only decision we can make that can keep us from reaching God's goals in our lives.

A GOAL IS A DREAM WITH A DEADLINE.

In Habakkuk 2:2 the Lord tells the prophet, ...*Write the vision, and make it plain upon tables, that he may run that readeth it.* The key to successful goal-setting is revealed in this scripture.

First, the vision must be written down. When you keep a vision in your mind, it is not really a goal; it is really nothing more than a dream. There is power in putting that dream down on paper. When you commit something to writing, commitment to achievement naturally follows. You can't start a fire with paper alone, but writing something down on paper can start a fire inside of you.

God Himself followed His Word here, by taking His vision for us and having it put down on paper in the form of the Bible. He did not just rely on the Holy Spirit to guide and direct us; He put His goals down in writing. We are told to make the word of the Lord plain upon "tables" (tablets) so that it is clear and specific as to what the vision is ". . . so that he may run that readeth it."

The key word is "run." God desires that we run with the vision and goal in our life. As long as we are running with the vision, we won't turn around. When you walk with a vision, it's easy to change directions and go the wrong way. **You can't stroll to a goal.**

In Proverbs 24:3,4 (TLB), we read: *Any enterprise is built by wise planning, becomes strong through common sense, and profits wonderfully by keeping abreast of the facts.* Simply stated, effective goal-setting and planning provides an opportunity to bring the future to the present and deal with it today. You will find that achievement is easy when your outer goals become an inner commitment.

Even though we have the Holy Spirit, we still need to prepare; we are just better equipped to do so. God's first choice for us in any situation cannot be disorder and waste of funds or resources. That's why proper planning is so important. Plan to the potential. Believe for God's biggest dream. When you plan, look to the future, not the past. You can't drive forward by looking out the rear window.

Always involve yourself with something that's bigger than you are, because that's where God is. Every great success was, at the beginning, impossible. We all have opportunity for success in our lives. It takes just as much energy and effort for a bad life as it does for a good life; yet most people live meaningless lives simply because they never decided to write their vision down and then follow through on it. Know this, if you can't see the mark, you can't press towards it.

Ponder the path of thy feet, and let all thy ways be established (Prov. 4:26). You will find that what you learn on the path to your goals is actually more valuable than achieving the goal itself. Columbus discovered America while searching for a route to India. Be on the lookout for the "Americas" in your path. Put God's vision for your life on paper, and begin to run with His plan.

SMILE. IT ADDS TO YOUR FACE VALUE.

Christians should be the happiest, most enthusiastic, people on earth. In fact, the word *enthusiasm* comes from a Greek word, *entheous* which means "God within" or "full of God."

Smiling — being happy and enthusiastic — is always a choice and not a result. It is a decision that must be consciously made. Enthusiasm and joy and happiness will improve your personality and people's opinion of you. It will help you keep a proper perspective on life. Helen Keller said, "Keep your face to the sunshine and you cannot see the shadow."

The bigger the challenge you are facing, the more enthusiasm you need. Philippians 2:5 (NIV) says, *Your attitude should be the same as that of Christ Jesus.* I believe Jesus was a man Who had a smile on His face, a spring in His step, and joy on His countenance.

Our attitude always tells others what we expect in return.

A smile is a powerful weapon. It can even break the ice. You'll find that being happy and enthusiastic is like a head cold — it's very, very contagious. A laugh a day will keep negative people away. You will also find that as enthusiasm increases, stress and fear in your life will decrease. The Bible says that the joy of the Lord is our strength. (Neh. 8:10.)

Many people say, "Well, no wonder that person is happy, confident, and positive; if I had his job and assets, I would be too." Such thinking falsely assumes that successful people are positive because they have a good income and lots of possessions. But the reverse is true. Such people probably have a good income and lots of possessions as a result of being positive, confident, and happy.

Enthusiasm always motivates to action. No significant accomplishment has ever been made without enthusiasm. In John 15:10,11 (NIV) we have a promise from the Lord, *"If you obey my commands, you will remain in my love, just as I have obeyed my Father's commands and remain in his love. I have told you this so that my joy may be in you and that your joy may be complete."*

The joy and love of the Lord are yours — so smile!

AN ALIBI IS JUST A LIE.

Quitting, giving up, failing, judging — all these begin with an excuse. Never allow an obstacle in your life to become an alibi — which is simply egotism turned the wrong side out.

You, therefore, have no excuse, you who pass judgment on someone else, for at whatever point you judge the other, you are condemning yourself, because you who pass judgment do the same things (Rom. 2:1 NIV). We Christians should be people who make progress, not excuses. When we alibi, we always point the blame somewhere else. This causes further judgment to come our way.

There have always been people who have tried to make excuses to the Lord. Some knew that their alibis were not true. And then there were those who made excuses and actually believed them; these ended up in much different circumstances.

In Luke 14:18-20 (NIV) Jesus told a parable of the great end-time banquet and the men who were invited to the Lord's table:

"But they all alike began to make excuses. The first said, 'I have just bought a field, and I must go to see it. Please excuse me.'

45

"Another said, 'I have just bought five yoke of oxen, and I'm on my way to try them out. Please excuse me.'

"Still another said, 'I just got married, so I can't come.' "

These men alibied and missed out on salvation. All of them made the mistake of believing their alibis rather than God.

Two other men in the Bible, Moses and Gideon, also made excuses to the Lord. The difference is that, although they alibied, they recognized that their excuses were not the truth. Moses tried to alibi to God. In Exodus 4:10-12 (NIV), he said:

...*"O Lord, I have never been eloquent, neither in the past nor since you have spoken to your servant. I am slow of speech and tongue."*

The Lord said to him, "Who gave man his mouth? Who makes him deaf or dumb? Who gives him sight or makes him blind? Is it not I, the Lord? Now go; I will help you speak and will teach you what to say."

Gideon, in Judges 6:15 (NIV), argued:

"But Lord,...how can I save Israel? My clan is the weakest in Manasseh, and I am the least in my family."

The Lord answered, "I will be with you, and you will strike down the Midianites as if they were but one man."

When you are confronted with an alibi, do as Moses and Gideon: choose to believe God, and not the excuse. In John 15:22 (NIV), Jesus said, *"If I had not come and spoken to them, they would not be guilty of sin. Now, however, they have no excuse for their sin."*

Recognize an alibi for what it is — a sin against God.

DON'T QUIT AFTER A VICTORY.

There are two times when a person stops: after a defeat and after a victory. Eliminating this kind of procrastination increases momentum.

Robert Schuller has a good saying: "Don't cash in, cast into deeper water." Don't stop after a success, keep the forward momentum going.

One of the great prizes of victory is the opportunity to do more. The trouble is, we've innoculated ourselves with small doses of success which keep us from catching the real thing.

As I was writing this section on momentum, I couldn't get out of my mind a picture of a large boulder at the top of a hill. This boulder represents our lives. If we rock the boulder back and forth and get it moving, its momentum will make it almost unstoppable. The same is true of us.

The Bible promises us God's divine momentum in our lives. In Philippians 1:6 the Apostle Paul writes, *Being confident of this very thing, that he which hath begun a good work in you will perform it until the day of Jesus Christ.* God's momentum always results in growth.

There are five ways to have divine momentum in your life:

1. Be fruitful. (2 Cor. 9:10.)
2. Speak the truth. (Eph. 4:15.)
3. Be spiritually mature. (Heb. 6:1.)
4. Crave the Word of God. (1 Pet. 2:2.)
5. Grow in the grace and knowledge of Jesus. (2 Pet. 3:18.)

God's definition of spiritual momentum is found in 2 Peter 1:5 (NIV):

For this very reason, make every effort to add to your faith goodness; and to goodness, knowledge; and to knowledge, self-control; and to self-control, perseverance; and to perseverance, godliness; and to godliness, brotherly kindness; and to brotherly kindness, love. For if you possess these qualities in increasing measure, they will keep you from being ineffective and unproductive in your knowledge of our Lord Jesus Christ.

Let go of whatever makes you stop.

THE BEST HELPING HAND
YOU WILL EVER FIND
IS AT THE END OF YOUR OWN ARM.

One of the biggest lies of the world is that we are not responsible for our own actions. We are told that it's our mother's fault, our employer's fault, our neighbor's fault, the government's fault, society's fault. But in Romans 14:12, the Bible clearly indicates who is responsible and accountable for our deeds: *So then every one of us shall give account of himself to God.*

We may want or even attempt to shift the blame to others, but there is no escaping the truth: when we point the finger at someone else, there are three fingers pointing back at ourselves.

Throughout my career as a consultant, I have met with many businessmen who were looking everywhere for answers. It was amazing to me how many were anxiously searching for help from other people while they had — between them and God — everything they needed to succeed. They were easily willing to give up control of their vision to others in exchange for money or even companionship. Their mistake was in looking to others instead of God.

This kind of false security invariably leads to imbalanced relationships which eventually result in destruction of the person and his dream.

Now I believe that God sends people across our path to bless us and help us. But we should be directed by God and be very cautious when entering into any partnership relationship. We must be sure that the reason for the relationship is right; that it is not an attempt to compromise or look for a shortcut.

For every successful partnership, there are hundreds that were disasters. Exercise great caution when affiliating with someone else. In Exodus, God gave Moses some good advice that is applicable to us as Christians today. He said, *"Be careful not to make a treaty with those who live in the land where you are going, or they will be a snare among you"* (Ex. 34:12 NIV).

I believe that most of the things God wants to teach us, He wants us to learn for ourselves. Mark Twain said, "A man who carries a cat by the tail learns something he can learn no other way."

Decide for yourself. Learn for yourself. Answer for yourself.

THE MOST NATURAL THING TO DO WHEN YOU GET KNOCKED DOWN IS TO GET UP.

How we respond to failure and mistakes is one of the most important decisions we make every day. Failure doesn't mean that nothing has been accomplished. There is always the opportunity to learn something. What is in you will always be bigger than whatever is around you.

We all experience failure and make mistakes. In fact, successful people always have more failure in their lives than average people do. You will find that throughout history all great people, at some point in their lives, have failed. **Only those who do not expect anything are never disappointed. Only those who never try, never fail.** Anyone who is currently achieving anything in life is simultaneously risking failure. It is always better to fail in doing something than to excel in doing nothing. A flawed diamond is more valuable than a perfect brick. People who have no failures also have few victories.

Everybody gets knocked down, it's how fast he gets up that counts. There is a positive correlation between spiritual maturity and how quickly a person responds to his failures and mistakes. The greater the degree of spiritual maturity, the greater the ability to get back up and go on. The less the spiritual maturity, the longer the individual will continue to hang on to past failures. Every person knows someone who, to this day, is still held back by mistakes he made years ago. God never sees any of us as failures; He only sees us as learners.

We have only failed when we do not learn from the experience. The decision is up to us. We can choose to turn a failure into a hitching post, or a guidepost.

Here is the key to being free from the stranglehold of past failures and mistakes: learn the lesson and forget the details. Gain from the experience, but do not roll over and over in your mind the minute details of it. Build on the experience, and get on with your life.

Remember: **the call is higher than the fall.**

THOSE WHO DON'T TAKE CHANCES DON'T MAKE ADVANCES.

All great discoveries have been made by people whose faith ran ahead of their minds. Significant achievements have not been obtained by taking small risks on unimportant issues. Don't ever waste time planning, analyzing, and risking on small ideas. It is always wise to spend more time on decisions that are irreversible and less time on those that are reversible.

Learn to stretch, to reach out where God is. Aim high and take risks. The world's approach is to look to next year based on last year. We Christians need to reach to the potential, not reckon to the past. Those who make great strides are those who take chances and plan toward the challenges of life.

Don't become so caught up in small matters that you can't take advantage of important opportunities. Most people spend their entire lives letting down buckets into empty wells. They continue to waste away their days trying to draw them up again.

Choose today to dream big, to strive to reach the full potential of your calling. Choose to major on the important issues of life, not on the unimportant. H. Stern said, "If you're hunting rabbits in tiger country, you must keep your eye peeled for tigers, but when you are hunting tigers you can ignore the rabbits." There are plenty of tigers to go around. Don't be distracted by or seek after the rabbits of life. Set your sights on "big game."

Security and opportunity are total strangers. If an undertaking doesn't include faith, it's not worthy of being called God's direction. I don't believe that God would call any of us to do anything that would not include an element of faith in Him.

There is a famous old saying that goes, "Even a turtle doesn't get ahead unless he sticks his neck out." **Dream big, because you serve a big God.**

"REMEMBER THAT THE FAITH TO MOVE MOUNTAINS ALWAYS CARRIES A PICK."
— ANONYMOUS QUOTE

Rising above mediocrity never just happens, it is always a result of faith combined with works.

Faith without works is like gold within the earth. It is of no value until it is worked and mined out. **A person who has faith without actions is like a bird with wings but no feet.** In James 2:17 the Bible says, *Even so faith, if it hath not works, is dead, being alone.*

Biblical principles times nothing equals nothing.

We believers need to be people who put our faith into action. One individual with faith and action constitutes a majority. Don't wait for your ship to come in — swim out to it. Thomas Edison said it best when he noted, "Opportunity is missed by most people because it is dressed in overalls and looks like work." True faith has hands and feet; it takes action. It's not enough to "know that you know." It's more important to *show* that you know.

The word *work* appears in the Bible 564 times. So work is not a vague scriptural concept. When faith and works operate together, the result is a masterpiece. We should choose to keep our faith working all the time and not quit. George Bernard Shaw said, "When I was young

I observed that nine out of every ten things I did were failures. So I did ten times more work."

The founder of Holiday Inns, Kemin Wilson, when asked how he became successful, replied, "I really don't know why I'm here. I never got a degree, and I've only worked half days my entire life. I guess my advice is to do the same, work half days every day. And it doesn't matter which half. The first twelve hours or the second twelve hours." Tap into the power that is produced when faith is mixed with action, and then watch God move in your situation.

PART II:
LOOKING OUTWARD

BEING A SERVANT WON'T MAKE YOU FAMOUS, JUST RICH.

Some time ago I received a telephone call. When I answered the phone, the voice on the other end of the line said: "Bang! You're dead!" I paused. I didn't quite know what to think about what had been said to me. Then I heard a familiar voice, that of James Campbell, a client of mine: "John, just calling to remind you that we all need to die to ourselves every day."

That is true. There is always room at the top for anyone who is willing to say, "I'll serve."

Several years ago I was listening to Zig Ziglar. In his presentation, he said, "You'll always have everything in life that you want, if you'll help enough other people get what they want." When I heard that statement, something went off on the inside to me. Then and there I made a conscious decision to incorporate that concept into my life. It has made a tremendous difference.

True Christian leadership always begins with servanthood.

Selfishness always ends in self-destruction. John Ruskin said, "When a man is wrapped up in himself, he makes a pretty small package."

Being a servant is not always the most natural thing to do. You know, we are all conditioned to think about ourselves. That's why 97 percent of all people, when offered a new pen to try out, will write their own names. Yet despite our tendency toward self-promotion, it is always true that more is accomplished when nobody cares who gets the credit.

God has always called us to serve those whom we lead. Be willing to serve, without trying to reap the benefits. Before looking for a way to get, look for ways to give.

No one is truly a success in life until he has learned how to serve. The old saying is true: "The way to the throne room is through the servant's quarters." One of the most powerful decisions you can make in your life is to do something for someone who doesn't have the power or resources to return the favor. In Matthew 23:11 our Lord said: *...he that is greatest among you shall be your servant.* And in Matthew 20:26,27 He declared:

But it shall not be so among you: but whosoever will be great among you, let him be your minister;

And whosoever will be chief among you, let him be your servant.

One of the most incredible benefits of being a Christian is the fact that when you give of yourself to help other people, you cannot help but be personally and abundantly rewarded. The rewards and blessings of being a servant always extend far beyond what can be seen or heard.

YOUR BEST FRIENDS ARE THOSE WHO BRING OUT THE BEST IN YOU.

We need to be careful of the kind of insulation we use in our lives. We need to insulate ourselves from negative people and ideas. But, we should never insulate ourselves from Godly counsel and wisdom.

It is a fact that misery wants your company. In Proverbs 27:19 (TLB) we read, *A mirror reflects a man's face, but what he is really like is shown by the kind of friends he chooses.* Proverbs 13:20 tells us, *He that walketh with wise men shall be wise: but a companion of fools shall be destroyed.* We become like those with whom we associate.

Some years ago I found myself at a stagnation point in my life. I was unproductive and unable to see clearly God's direction. One day I noticed that almost all of my friends were in the same situation. When we got together, all we talked about was our problems. As I prayed about this matter, God showed me that He desired that I have "foundational-level" people in my life. Such people who bring out the best in us, those who influence us to become better people ourselves. They cause us to have greater faith and confidence, to see things from God's perspective. After being with them, our spirits and our sights are raised.

I have found that **it is better to be alone than in the wrong company.** A single conversation with the right person can be more valuable than many years of study.

The Lord showed me that I needed to change my closest associations, that there were some other people I needed to have contact with on a regular basis. These were men and women of great faith, those who made me a better person just by being around them. They were the ones who saw the gifts in me and could correct me in a constructive, loving way. My choice to change my closest associations was a turning point in my life.

When you surround yourself and affiliate with the right kind of people, you enter into the God-ordained power of agreement. Ecclesiastes 4:9,10,12 (TLB) states:

Two can accomplish more than twice as much as one, for the results can be much better. If one falls, the other pulls him up; but if a man falls when he is alone, he's in trouble.

And one standing alone can be attacked and defeated, but two can stand back-to-back and conquer; three is even better, for a triple-braided cord is not easily broken.

You need to steer clear of negative-thinking "experts." **Remember: in the eyes of average people average is always considered outstanding.** Look carefully at the closest associations in your life, for that is the direction you are heading.

WE ARE CALLED TO STAND OUT, NOT BLEND IN.

A majority, many times, is a group of highly motivated snails. If a thousand people say something foolish, it's still foolish. Truth is never dependent upon consensus of opinion.

In 1 Peter 2:9, the Bible says of us Christians, ...ye *are a chosen generation, a royal priesthood, an holy nation, a peculiar people; that ye should shew forth the praises of him who hath called you out of darkness into his marvellous light.* Romans 12:2 exhorts us, *And be not conformed to this world, but be ye transformed by the renewing of your mind, that ye may prove what is that good, and acceptable, and perfect, will of God.*

One of the greatest compliments that anybody can give you is to say that you are different. We Christians live in this world, but we are aliens. We should talk differently, act differently, and perform differently. We are called to stand out.

There should be something different about you. If you don't stand out in a group, if there is not something unique or different in your life, you should re-evaluate yourself.

One way to stand head and shoulders above the crowd is to choose to do regular, ordinary things in an extraordinary and supernatural way with great enthusiasm. God has always done some of His very best work through remnants, when the circumstances appear to be stacked against them. In fact, in every battle described in the Bible, God was always on the side of the "underdog," the minority.

Majority rule is not always right. It is usually those people who don't have dreams or visions of their own who want to take a vote. People in groups tend to agree on courses of action that they as individuals know are not right.

Don't be persuaded or dissuaded by group opinion. It doesn't make any difference whether anyone else believes, you must believe. **Never take direction from a crowd for your personal life. And never choose to quit just because somebody else disagrees with you.** In fact, the two worst things you can say to yourself when you get an idea is: 1) "That has never been done before," and 2) "That has been done before." Just because somebody else has gone a particular way and not succeeded does not mean that you too will fail.

Be a pioneer, catch a few arrows, and stand out.

TODAY IS THE DAY TO DECIDE TO GO THROUGH WHAT YOU'VE BEEN GOING THROUGH.

S top talking constantly about the situation you are "going through." Decide today to get on through it! What do I mean by this statement? I mean, **don't accept your present, temporary situation as your future, permanent situation.** Despite your current circumstances, make up your mind to get on with your life and fulfill your divine purpose and calling.

God wants each of us to come through whatever situations we may face in life. We are not to be moved by what we see, but by what we do not see. This is what the Apostle Paul meant when he wrote that we walk by faith, not by sight. (2 Cor. 5:7.) Today is the day to begin to walk by faith — right out of your present circumstances!

If you have been saying for years, "I'm going through this situation," you need to change your story. Begin to declare: "I've had enough! Now is the time I'm going to get through this mess!"

The Bible contains many promises which can deliver you today. If you will believe and appropriate these promises, you will begin to see your circumstances line up with the Word and will of God — eventually, if not immediately.

You see, it's the devil who tells us that we will never be victorious, that we will never go through what we're going through. But in 1 Corinthians 10:13 (NIV) we are told, *No temptation has seized you except what is common to man. And God is faithful; he will not let you be tempted beyond what you can bear. But when you are tempted, he will also provide a way out so that you can stand up under it.*

This is your verse to take hold of and stand on. God is faithful. He will provide a way out. So you can take your stand of faith and boldly proclaim, "I'm going to go through with what I've been going through!" Natural circumstances may still remain unchanged, but between you and God, you are already through that situation.

Some people stay in the same hopeless situation their whole lives, never making a firm decision to seek God and His power to get through the circumstances they face. The commandment for us to be longsuffering does not require us to stay in a miserable situation one second longer than is absolutely necessary. Here's how we poise ourselves to break through: *And be not conformed to this world, but be ye transformed by the renewing of your mind, that ye may prove what is that good, and acceptable, and perfect, will of God* (Rom. 12:2). Be transformed by renewing your mind to the Word of God. Then you will know what is the good and perfect will of the Lord, and will be able to go through — once and for all — what you've been going through so long.

SAY NO TO MANY GOOD IDEAS.

One of the tricks of the devil is to get us to say yes to too many things. Then we end up being spread so thin that we are mediocre in everything and excellent in nothing.

There is one guaranteed formula for failure, and that is to try to please everyone.

There is a difference between something that is good and something that is right. Oftentimes, it is a challenge for many people to discern that which is good from that which is right. As Christians, our higher responsibility is always to do the right things. These come first. We should do the things that we're called to do, the things that are right, with excellence, first — before we start diversifying into other areas.

There comes a time in every person's life when he must learn to say no to many good ideas. In fact, the more an individual grows, the more opportunities he will have to say no. Becoming focused is a key to results. Perhaps no other virtue is so overlooked as a key to growth and success. The temptation is always to do a little bit of everything.

Saying no to a good idea doesn't always mean never. No may mean not right now.

There is power in the word *no*. No is an anointed word, one which can break the yoke of overcommitment and weakness. No can be used to turn a situation from bad to good, from wrong to right. Saying no can free you from burdens that you really don't need to carry right now.

It can also allow you to devote the correct amount of attention and effort to God's priorities in your life.

I'm sure that as you read the title of this nugget, past experiences and present situations come to mind. I'm sure you recall many situations in which no or not right now would have been the right answer. Don't put yourself through that kind of disappointment in the future.

Yes and no are the two most important words that you will ever say. These are the two words that determine your destiny in life. How and when you say them affects your entire future.

Saying no to lesser things can mean saying yes to the priorities in your life.

THERE IS ALWAYS FREE FOOD
ON A FISH HOOK.

Did you know that the best shortcut you can ever take is to do what God says, in His timing? Shortcuts outside of the will of God invite compromise and create strife and confusion.

We believers need to understand that we are long-distance runners. We are marathoners. We are not on a sprint. We do not need to look for get-rich-quick schemes or shortcuts that open the door to compromise.

There is an old saying that is absolutely true: "If you keep your attention on learning the tricks of the trade, you will never learn the trade." Watch out for fads, even spiritual fads because the letters of the word fad stand for "For A Day."

There is a story told of a beautiful bird that was known for its great singing. It would sit at the top of a tree and make all kinds of lovely melodies. One day a man was walking through the woods. He passed by the tree and heard this beautiful bird singing. The bird saw the man and perceived that he was holding a box.

"What do you have in the box?" he asked the man.

The man replied that he had large, juicy earthworms in the box. "I will sell you a worm for one of your beautiful feathers," he offered.

The bird reached down, pulled out a feather, and gave it in exchange for a worm. Then he took the worm and ate it. He reflected to himself, "Why should I have to work so hard to get a worm when it's so easy to get one this way?"

Well, this affair continued over a period of many days and soon the bird no longer had any beautiful feathers to use to pay for worms. Furthermore, he could no longer fly, nor was he pretty any longer. So he didn't feel like singing beautiful songs any more. He was a very unwise and unhappy bird.

Like this foolish bird, we are always subject to the temptation to look for shortcuts, ways to get ahead and obtain the things we want and the results we desire. But, as this poor creature learned to his regret, there is a price associated with taking shortcuts.

Eventually, we will learn that there is no shortcut to success. One of the hidden truths of life is the fact that the path to the prize is always more valuable than the prize itself. Shortcuts rob us of those valuable lessons that we need to learn along the way. When presented with an option of a shortcut, a way that is not of God, say no. Be persistent and stick to the path on which the Lord has placed you.

Yes, it's true: **we must stay on the path of the circumference of time before we arrive at the center of opportunity.**

WHEN YOU REFUSE TO CHANGE, YOU END UP IN CHAINS.

We humans are custom-built for change.

Inanimate objects like clothes, houses, and buildings don't have the ability to truly change. They grow out of style and become unusable. But at any point in time, at any age, any one of us is able to change. To change doesn't always mean to do the opposite. In fact, most of the time, it means to add on to or slightly adjust.

When we are called upon by the Lord to change, we will continue to reach toward the same goal, but perhaps in a slightly different way. When we refuse to cooperate with the change that God is requiring of us, we make chains that constrain and restrict us.

There are three things that we know about the future: 1) it is not going to be like the past, 2) it is not going to be exactly the way we think it's going to be, and 3) the rate of change will take place faster than we imagine. The Bible indicates that in the end times in which we are now living, changes will come about much quicker than ever before in history.

In 1803 the British created a civil service position in which a man was required to stand on the cliffs of Dover with a spy glass. His job was to be on the lookout for invasion. He was to ring a bell if he saw the army of Napoleon Bonaparte approaching. Now that was all well and good for the time, but that job was not eliminated until 1945! How many spy glasses on the cliffs of Dover are we still holding onto in our lives? **We should choose not to allow "the way we've always done it" to cause us to miss opportunities God is providing for us today.**

Even the most precious of all gems needs to be chiseled and faceted to achieve its best luster. There is nothing that remains so constant as change. Don't end up like concrete, all mixed up and permanently set.

In Isaiah 42:9, the Lord declares: *Behold, the former things are come to pass, and new things do I declare: before they spring forth I tell you of them.* The Bible is a book that tells us how to respond to change ahead of time. You see, I believe that we can decide in advance how we will respond to most situations. When I was coaching basketball many years ago, I used to tell my players that most situations in a game can be prepared for ahead of time. We used to practice different game situations so that when the players got into an actual game situation they would know how to respond. **One of the main reasons the Bible was written was to prepare us ahead of time, to teach us how to respond in advance to many of the situations that we will encounter in life.**

Choose to flow with God's plan. Be sensitive to the new things He is doing. Stay flexible to the Holy Spirit and know that ours is a God who directs, adjusts, moves, and corrects us. He is always working to bring us into perfection.

EVERYTHING BIG STARTS WITH SOMETHING LITTLE.

❧

All of God's great people in the Bible were faithful in the small things. In Matthew 25 Jesus told the parable of the talents. In it He referred to the one servant who had taken his master's money and multiplied it. In verse 23 his master said to that man, *...Well done, good and faithful servant; thou hast been faithful over a few things, I will make thee ruler over many things: enter thou into the joy of thy lord.* In Zechariah 4:10 the Lord asks the prophet, *For who hath despised the day of small things?....* There is a powerful principle in taking small steps.

Many people are not moving with God today simply because they were not willing to take the small steps He placed before them. If you have received a call into any particular area, you should leap at the opportunity — no matter how small — to move in the direction in which the Lord has called you. If you are called to be a youth pastor, and are sitting at home waiting for an invitation from some large church, you should know that it will never come. You need to find the first young person you can, put your arm around him, and begin to minister to him.

Don't be afraid to take small steps. The Bible promises us that if we are faithful in small matters, one day we will be rulers over many larger things.

The impossible, many times, is just simply the untried.

I can remember a time in my life when I was literally frozen with fear at what God had called me to do. It seemed so huge a task that I was unable to bring myself to face it. A friend came to me and spoke two words that broke that paralysis in my life. He said simply, "Do something!" If you are at a point of paralysis in your life because of what God wants you to do, the word for you today is "Do something!" Don't worry about the goal, just take the steps that take you past the starting point and soon you'll get to a point of no return. As you climb higher, you'll be able to see much farther.

We should all learn to grow wherever we're planted.

As you begin, don't be afraid. Eric Hoffer said: "Fear of becoming a has-been keeps some people from becoming anything." Every great idea is impossible from where you are starting today. But little goals add up, and they add up rapidly. Most people don't succeed because they are too afraid even to try. They don't begin because of that old fear of failure.

Many times the final goal seems so unreachable that it keeps us from even making an effort. But, once you've made your decision and have started, you are more than half-way there. God will begin with you today — no matter what your circumstances. Just think how thankful you would be if you lost everything you have right now and then got it all back again. Wouldn't you be ready to go? Choose to think eternally, but act daily.

A CHIP ON THE
SHOULDER WEIGHS A TON.

Forgiveness is essential for good human relationships. You cannot give a hug with your arms folded.

Forgiveness of others also assures us of God's forgiveness of our own faults and failures. In Matthew 6:14,15 (NIV) Jesus said, *"For if you forgive men when they sin against you, your heavenly Father will also forgive you. But if you do not forgive men their sins, your Father will not forgive your sins."* The weight of unforgiveness greatly drags a person down. It is a tremendous load to carry in the race that we Christians are called to run.

When faced with the decision to forgive and forget, never make the excuse, "But no one knows what that person did to me!" That may be true, but the question is: do you know what unforgiveness will do to you?

What really matters is what happens in us not to us.

Unforgiveness leads to great bitterness, which is a deadly misuse of the creative flow from above. Great amounts of mental energy and brain power are used up in pondering over a negative situation and plotting how to "get even." This kind of thinking is totally unproductive. People who make a habit of burning bridges will discover that it is they who have been left isolated and alone and that they will deal with neutrals and enemies the rest of their lives. That's why we should build bridges, not burn them. Vengeance is a poor traveling companion. Every Christian is called to a ministry of reconciliation. (2 Cor. 5:18.) Getting even always causes imbalance and unhappiness in a life.

As I have worked with churches throughout America, in every stagnating situation I have found areas of unforgiveness. And conversely, I have found that, generally speaking, churches which are growing don't talk about past problems.

Never underestimate the power of forgiveness to loose and free you to accomplish your goals and fulfill your calling. It is the one power you have over a person who slanders or criticizes you. **The farther you walk in forgiveness, the greater the distance you put between yourself and the negative situation.**

Forgiveness gives you a spring in your spiritual walk and a second wind in the race of life.

NEVER SURRENDER YOUR DREAM TO NOISY NEGATIVES.

Nobody can ever make you feel average without your permission. Ingratitude and criticism are going to come; they are a part of the price paid for leaping past mediocrity.

Jesus Himself, after healing the ten lepers, was only thanked by one of them. (Luke 17:11-19.) Instead of being surprised by ingratitude from others, we should learn to expect it.

If you move with God, you will be criticized. **The only sure way to fend off criticism is to do nothing and be nothing.** Those who do things inevitably stir up criticism.

But the Bible offers this great promise concerning criticism: **the truth always outlives a lie.** This fact is backed up by Proverbs 12:19: *The lip of truth shall be established for ever: but a lying tongue is but for a moment.* Also, in Hebrews 13:6 we are told ...*that we may boldly say, The Lord is my helper, and I will not fear what man shall do unto me.*

We should never judge a person by what is said of him by his enemies. Kenneth Tynan has provided the best description of a critic I have ever heard. "A critic," he said, "is a man who knows the way but can't drive the car." **We Christians are not called to respond to criticism; we are called to respond to God.** Often, criticism will present the best platform from which to proclaim the truth.

Most of the time people who are critical are either jealous or uninformed. They usually say things that have no impact whatsoever upon the truth. There's a famous anonymous saying that describes this situation perfectly: "It is useless for the sheep to pass resolutions in favor of vegetarianism while the wolf remains of a different opinion." If what you say and do is of God, it will not make any difference if every person on the face of the earth stands up and criticizes. Likewise, if it is not of God, nothing other people say will make it right.

Pay no attention to negative criticism. *Trust in the Lord, and do good...*(Ps. 37:3) knowing that in the end what you do in the Lord will be rewarded.

YOUR PROBLEM IS YOUR PROMOTION.

Every obstacle introduces a person to himself.

How we respond to obstacles in our path is important.

The greatest example of an obstacle in the Bible is the giant Goliath who confronted and intimidated the armies of Israel, including the brothers of a young shepherd lad man named David. Of course, we know that David's brothers chose not to do anything about the obstacle before them, but David did. The difference between David and his brothers was this: the brothers looked at the obstacle and figured it was too big to hit, but David looked at the obstacle and figured it was too big to miss.

The way you look at any obstacle in your life makes all the difference.

Let each new obstacle force you to go to the next level in God. **No obstacle will ever leave you the way it found you.** You will either be better or you will be worse as a result of that confrontation.

But keep in mind one important fact about obstacles: every obstacle has a limited lifespan. Many times there are things that we worried about last year that we can't even remember today. One of the biggest lies of the devil is that things will not change, that they will not pass.

Mediocre people tend to be tamed and subdued by obstacles, but great leaders always rise above them. You and I need to be like the great man, who, when asked what helped him overcome the obstacles of life, responded, "The other obstacles." We should be like a kite that rises against the wind, causing it to mount higher and higher. Every problem has a soft spot — there is an answer.

Since many of the obstacles we face are money related, the correct perspective is to know that if a problem can be solved with a checkbook, it's not really an obstacle; it's an expense.

Someone has said that obstacles are what we see when we take our eyes off the goal. Keep your eyes on the goal and remember that you are not alone in your struggle for *...we know that in all things God works for the good of those who love him, who have been called according to his purpose* (Rom. 8:28 NIV).

Really, **in times of adversity you don't have an obstacle to deal with, you have a choice to make.** In the midst of unbelievable circumstances, believe.

IF IN DOUBT, DON'T.

One day a hunter came across a bear in the woods. The bear said to the hunter, "I want a full stomach."

The hunter responded, "I want a fur coat."

"Let's compromise," suggested the bear — and promptly ate the man. As a result, they both got what they wanted. The bear went away with a full stomach and the man went away wrapped in fur.

This hunter learned the lesson of compromise: **when having to choose between the lesser of two evils, choose neither.**

In Deuteronomy 30:19 (NIV) the Lord says to His people, *This day I call heaven and earth as witnesses against you that I have set before you life and death, blessings and curses. Now choose life, so that you and your children may live.* You and I have a choice. Every day we must choose between life and death. We should never settle for just anything; we should always seek the best. The fact is that it is rarely the strong man who urges compromise. A compromise will always be more expensive than either of the alternatives.

The call of God is always a call to excellence — never a call to mediocrity. If anything is worth doing at all, it is worth doing well. If you can't do it with excellence, don't bother. Someone has said, "If you don't have time to do it right, when will you have time to do it over?"

When compromise is allowed in one area, it always leaks out and begins to affect other areas. It also allows lies, deceit, and error to creep into a life and take it over. I know people who have turned from the Lord completely. Their troubles all started because of compromises at work. They began to give in on little things, which soon became bigger things. It wasn't long before compromise had begun to infiltrate their personal life, then their home life. Eventually it overtook and overwhelmed them.

In Proverbs 4:26,27, the writer warns us:

Ponder the path of thy feet, and let all thy ways be established.

Turn not to the right hand nor to the left: remove thy foot from evil.

Don't allow compromise to creep in and destroy. You can't say, "Well, I'll compromise in this one area and everything else will be okay." Once it has a foothold, compromise grows and spreads.

Be a person of integrity. Guard your reputation, and the reputation of Jesus Christ and His Church. If the only way others can tell that you are a Christian is by the symbol of the fish on your business card, do us all a favor and leave it off. Take a stand today against compromise.

"AN ARMY OF SHEEP LED BY A LION WOULD DEFEAT AN ARMY OF LIONS LED BY A SHEEP." — OLD ARAB PROVERB

What are the actions and attributes of a leader? What is it that makes him different from others?

1. A leader is always full of praise.
2. A leader learns to use the phrases "thank you" and "please" on his way to the top.
3. A leader is always growing.
4. A leader is possessed with his dreams.
5. A leader launches forth before success is certain.
6. A leader is not afraid of confrontation.
7. A leader talks about his own mistakes before talking about someone else's.
8. A leader is a person of honesty and integrity.
9. A leader has a good name.
10. A leader makes others better.
11. A leader is quick to praise and encourage the smallest amount of improvement.
12. A leader is genuinely interested in others.
13. A leader looks for opportunities to find someone doing something right.

14. A leader takes others up with him.

15. A leader responds to his own failures and acknowledges them before others have to discover and reveal them.

16. A leader never allows murmuring — from himself or others.

17. A leader is specific in what he expects.

18. A leaders holds accountable those who work with him.

19. A leader does what is right rather than what is popular.

20. A leader is a servant.

A leader is a lion, not a sheep.

MAKING OTHERS BETTER
IS A BOOMERANG.

A famous old poem goes like this:

"When days are hot and flies are thick, use horse sense
— cooperate.

This is a truth all horses know, they learned it many
centuries ago.

One tail on duty at the rear can reach that fly behind
the ear.

But two tails when arranged with proper craft can do
the job both fore and aft."

Your decision to bound past mediocrity will help
pull up others with you.

**Choosing God's will in our lives always affects
others and makes them better.** William Danforth said,
"Our most valuable possessions are those which can be
shared without lessening those which when shared
multiply. Our least valuable possessions are those which
when divided are diminished."

We should look for opportunities to invest of
ourselves in others and to help make them better.

Somebody did that for you once. Somebody saw
something in you and reached out to help you. That act
of kindness has determined where you are today. It may
have been your pastor, your parents, a friend, a teacher,

coach, neighbor, or just someone who offered some extra money, prayers, good advice, or equipment and supplies. But whoever it was, that individual had the foresight and the resources to invest in you and take a risk on your future.

I have a challenge for you. This week take a few minutes and send a note to those people who reached out and greatly affected your life. Also do this: take a few minutes and reach out to help someone else get ahead. You will find that this will be one of the most satisfying experiences you've had in a long time.

Proverbs 3:27 says, *Withhold not good from them to whom it is due, when it is in the power of thine hand to do it.* Invest in somebody today. Believe in that person. Offer support and encouragement. Help him come up to another level.

Try it, you'll like it! You'll also benefit from it!

People are born originals, but most die copies.

The call in your life is not a copy.

In this day of peer pressure, trends, and fads, we need to realize and accept that each person has been custom-made by God the Creator. Each of us has a unique and personal call upon our lives. We are to be our own selves and not copy other people.

Because I do a lot of work with churches, I come into contact with many different types of people. One time I talked over the phone with a pastor I had never met and who did not know me personally. We came to an agreement that I was to visit his church as a consultant. As we were closing our conversation and were setting a time to meet at the local airport, he asked me, "How will I know you when you get off the plane?"

"Oh, don't worry, pastor; I'll know you," I responded jokingly. "You all look alike."

The point of this humorous story is this: **be the person God has made YOU to be.**

The call of God upon our lives is the provision of God in our lives. We do not need to come up to the standards of anyone else. **The average person compares himself with others, but we Christians should always compare ourselves with the person God has called us**

to be. That is our standard — God's unique plan and design for our lives. How the Lord chooses to deal with others has nothing to do with our individual call in life or God's timing and direction for us.

You and I can always find someone richer than we are, poorer than we are, or with more or less ability than we have. But how other people are, what they have, and what happens in their lives, has no effect upon our call. In Galatians 6:4 (TLB) we are admonished: *Let everyone be sure that he is doing his very best, for then he will have the personal satisfaction of work well done, and won't need to compare himself with someone else.*

God made you a certain way. You are unique. You are one of a kind. To copy others is to cheat yourself out of the fullness of what God has called you to be and to do.

So, choose to accept and become the person God has made you to be. Tap into the originality and creative genius of God in your life.

TEN TRUISMS THAT AREN'T TRUE.

1. **T**he way to guarantee success is to work smarter, not harder.

This is a losing idea. You will find that effective leaders do both. They work smarter, and they work harder.

2. Activity equals accomplishment.

Activity is not accomplishment. Hard work is not results. We should not ask ourselves whether we're busy, but what we're busy about. We serve a God Who is interested in results.

3. Take care of things, and they will take care of you.

We should not take care, we should take control. If you don't take control of your own life, somebody else will.

4. If you want to be a success, you must pay the price.

You don't pay the price for success; you possess the price for success. The path to success belongs to you. It's not something that you have to give up in order to succeed.

5. Don't waste (kill) time.

Although this truism expresses a good thought, it is really not accurate. When you waste time, it is not time you are wasting, it is your very life.

6. If it's not broke, don't fix it.

That is not good advice. Even though things are working, many times they still can be significantly improved or modified.

7. What you see is what you get.

We Christians are commanded not to be moved by what we see but by the Word of God. We are to see the unseen in every situation of life.

8. He is a self-made man.

There is no such thing. A person can succeed only with the help of God and others.

9. Talk is cheap.

False. Talk is very expensive. What an individual says is ultimately what he gets — and what he pays for.

10. Practice makes perfect.

No, perfect practice makes perfect. Wrong practice leads to wrong habits. Perfect practice leads to perfect action. Make sure that whatever you do on a regular basis is right and correct.

PART III:
LOOKING UPWARD

STOP EVERY DAY AND LOOK AT THE SIZE OF GOD.

Who is God? What is His personality like? What are His character traits?

According to the Bible, He is everlasting, just, caring, holy, divine, omniscient, omnipotent, omni-present and sovereign. He is light, perfection, abundance, salvation, wisdom, and love. He is the Creator, Savior, Deliverer, Redeemer, Provider, Healer, Advocate, and Friend. Never forget Who lives inside of you: *...the Lord...the great God, the great King above all gods* (Ps. 95:3 NIV).

John, the beloved disciple, tells us: *Ye are of God, little children, and have overcome them: because greater is he that is in you, than he that is in the world* (1 John 4:4). Period. Exclamation point. That settles it!

God and the devil are not equal, just opposite.

I travel by air quite often and one of the benefits is that every time I fly I get a glimpse of God's perspective. I like looking at my challenges from 37,000 feet in the air. **No problem is too large for God's intervention, and no person is too small for God's attention.**

God is always able. If you don't need miracles, you don't need God. Dave Bordon, a friend of mine, said it best: "I don't understand the situation, but I understand God."

The miraculous realm of God always has to do with multiplication, not addition.

God likens our life in Him to seedtime and harvest. Do you realize how miraculous that is? Let me give you a conservative example: Suppose one kernel of corn produces one stalk with two ears, each ear having 200 kernels. From those 400 kernels come 400 stalks with 160,000 kernels. All from one kernel planted only one season earlier.

Our confession to the Lord should be Jeremiah 32:17 (NIV): *"Ah, Sovereign Lord, you have made the heavens and the earth by your great power and outstretched arm. Nothing is too hard for you."*

God is bigger than _____. Fill in the blank for your own life.

IDEAS GO AWAY, BUT DIRECTION STAYS.

How do you know the difference between what comes to your mind, and direction from God? There is a persistency to direction. The Bible says in Proverbs 19:21 (NIV), *Many are the plans in a man's heart, but it is the Lord's purpose that prevails.* In Psalm 32:8 the Lord promises, *I will instruct thee and teach thee in the way which thou shalt go: I will guide thee with mine eye.*

When we know what God wants us to do, then we can have total confidence that what we are attempting is right and that God is on our side. Direction is simply this: a stream with banks. And the most far-reaching, challenging direction is the most significant, because God is in it.

Direction is a matter of fact; ideas are a matter of opinion. One characteristic of direction from God is that it will always be humanly impossible to follow and fulfill alone without Him.

Direction is the mother of divine discomfort. We should have a certain divine discomfort at all times. A sensing that God is always wanting to direct us every day. A stirring in our hearts so that we are never quite satisfied spiritually with where we are in God or what we're doing for Him. We believers should be known as a people with a mission, not people just fishin'. Evangelist R.W. Schambach puts it this way: "Be called and sent, not up and went." We are a people with a purpose, not a problem.

God always calls us to and from. In Colossians 1:12,13 the Apostle Paul writes:

Giving thanks unto the Father, which hath made us meet to be partakers of the inheritance of the saints in light:

Who hath delivered us from the power of darkness, and hath translated us into the kingdom of his dear Son.

Be sure to look for areas God is calling you out of as well as in to. There is also a difference between God's will in our lives and God's will for our lives. God's will for our lives are those things that He intends for every person — salvation, strength, health, peace, joy, etc. But God's will in our lives is unique to each individual. One person may be called to live in one place all his life, while another is called to move six times within ten years.

Never be afraid of the light of God's direction. Maurice Freehill said, "Who is more foolish, a child afraid of the dark or the man afraid of the light?" Know this: wherever God guides, He provides. And where God calls, He appoints and anoints to do the work. Lay hold of those persistent directions in your life, and tap into the power of God's will for you.

RETREAT TO ADVANCE.

Sometimes the most important and urgent thing we can do is get away to a peaceful and anointed spot.

This is one of the most powerful concepts that I personally have incorporated into my life. I'm sitting right now writing this book in a cabin up on a hill overlooking a beautiful lake, miles away from the nearest city.

As we choose to draw away for a time, we can see and hear much more clearly about how to go ahead. Jesus did this many times during His earthly life, especially just before and after major decisions. The Bible says, ...in quietness and in confidence shall be your strength...(Is. 30:15). There's something invigorating and renewing about retreating to a quiet place of rest and peace. Silence is an environment in which great ideas are birthed.

There really are times when you should not see people, times when you should direct your whole attention toward God. I believe that every person should have a place of refuge, one out of the normal scope of living, one where he can "retreat to advance" and "focus in" with just the Lord and himself.

It is important to associate intently and as often as possible with your loftiest dreams. In Isaiah 40:31 we read, *But they that wait upon the Lord shall renew their strength; they shall mount up with wings as eagles; they shall run, and not be weary; and they shall walk, and not faint.* Learn to wait upon the Lord.

Make a regular appointment with yourself; it will be one of the most important you can ever have during the course of a week or a month. Choose to retreat to advance. See how much clearer you move forward with God as a result.

IT IS AS IMPORTANT
TO KNOW WHAT GOD CAN'T DO
AS TO KNOW WHAT HE CAN DO.

1. God cannot lie.
2. God cannot change.
3. God cannot recall our sins after we've asked for forgiveness.
4. God cannot be the author of confusion.
5. God cannot leave us or forsake us.
6. God cannot go back on His promises.
7. God cannot revoke His gifts.
8. God cannot be pleased without faith.
9. God cannot be defeated.
10. God cannot be too big for our problems.
11. God cannot be too little for our problems.
12. God cannot prefer one person over another.
13. God cannot break His covenant.
14. God cannot revoke His calling.
15. God cannot be unjust.
16. God cannot do anything contrary to the scriptures.
17. God cannot bless a lie.
18. God cannot love sin.

19. God cannot give anything to a double-minded man.
20. God cannot be forced into an impossible situation.
21. God cannot ignore the praises of His people.
22. God cannot be our problem.
23. God cannot be overcome by the world.
24. God cannot be late.
25. God cannot be neutral.
26. God cannot be weak.
27. God cannot bless doubt.
28. God cannot withhold wisdom from those who ask in faith.
29. God cannot be against us.
30. God cannot be limited or confined.

Have a ready will and walk, not idle time and talk.

A̲cting on God's will is like riding a bicycle: if you don't go on, you go off!

Once we know God's will and timing, we should be instant to obey, taking action without delay. Delay and hesitation when God is telling us to do something now is sin. The longer we take to act on whatever God wants us to do, the more unclear His directives become. We need to make sure that we are on God's interstate highway and not in a cul-de-sac.

Ours is a God of velocity. He is a God of timing and direction. These two always go together. It is never wise to act upon only one or the other. Jumping at the first opportunity seldom leads to a happy landing. In Proverbs 25:8 the writer tells us, *Go not forth hastily to strive, lest thou know not what to do in the end thereof, when thy neighbour hath put thee to shame.* A famous saying holds that people can be divided into three groups: 1) those who make things happen, 2) those who watch things happen, and 3) those who wonder what's happening. Even the right direction taken at the wrong time is a bad decision.

Most people miss out on God's best in their lives because they're not prepared. The Bible warns us that we should be prepared continually. The Apostle Paul exhorts us: *...be instant in season, out of season...* (2 Tim. 4:2).

There is a seasonality to God. In Ecclesiastes 3:1 we read: *To every thing there is a season, and a time to every purpose under the heaven.* Everything that you and I are involved in will have a spring (a time of planting and nurturing), a summer (a time of greatest growth), a fall (a time of harvest), and a winter (a time of decisions and planning).

Relax. Perceive, understand, and accept God's divine timing and direction.

THE BIBLE IS A BOOK OF COMMANDMENTS, NOT SUGGESTIONS.

The Bible does not offer suggestions; instead it commands us:

1. To be in right relationship with our brothers (Matt. 5:24)
2. To follow the rule of peace (Col. 3:15)
3. Not to "get even" (I Thess. 5:15)
4. To be an example to others (I Tim. 4:12)
5. To be abounding, steadfast and immovable (1 Cor. 15:58)
6. To renew our minds (Rom. 12:2)
7. To separate ourselves from unclean things (2 Cor. 6:17)
8. To be content with what we have (Heb. 13:5)
9. To be filled with the Spirit (Eph. 5:18)
10. To have no fear of what man can do to us (Luke 12:4)
11. Not to be like the world (Rom. 12:2)
12. To avoid greed and envy (Heb. 13:5)
13. To be patient with all people (1 Thess. 5:14)
14. Not to quit (2 Thess. 3:13)
15. To be people of quality (Heb. 6:12)
16. To beware of false prophets (Matt. 7:15)

17. To avoid wrong conversation (1 Tim. 6:20)
18. Not to quench the Spirit (1 Thess. 5:19)
19. To abstain from all lust of the flesh (1 Pet. 2:11)
20. To teach our children about the Lord (Eph. 6:4)
21. To cast all our cares upon the Lord (1 Pet. 5:7)
22. To avoid murmuring or disputing (Phil. 2:14)
23. To give thanks in everything (1 Thess. 5:18)
24. To give no place to the devil (Eph. 4:27)
25. Not to grieve the Holy Spirit (Eph. 4:30)
26. To honor our parents (Eph. 6:2; Matt. 19:19)
27. To submit ourselves to God (James 4:7)
28. To let men see our good works (Matt. 5:16)
29. To resist the devil (James 4:7)
30. To put on the whole armor of God (Eph. 6:11)
31. To humble ourselves (James 4:10)
32. To walk in the Spirit (Gal. 5:25)
33. To cast down vain imaginations (2 Cor. 10:5)
34. To come boldly to God (Heb. 4:16)
35. To seek God's kingdom and righteousness (Matt. 6:33)
36. To forsake not the assembling of ourselves (Heb 10:25)
37. To look to Jesus (Heb. 12:2)
38. To be in agreement (Matt. 18:19)
39. Not to cause others to stumble (Rom. 14:13)
40. To bless those who persecute us (Matt. 5:44)
41. To redeem the time (Eph. 5:16)
42. Not to be ashamed of Jesus (Rom. 10:11)
43. To have confidence in God (Heb. 10:35)
44. To worship decently and in order (1 Cor. 14:40)
45. To do all to God's glory (1 Cor. 10:31)

GOD'S CALL IS HEARD, NOT SEEN.

Just because an opportunity presents itself for which we are qualified does not necessarily mean that it is God's will for us to accept it. Many times circumstances "line up" and everything looks good, yet it doesn't seem right. In such cases, we need to hear from God. That's why I say that divine direction is really heard and not seen. We Christians should be more interested in the unseen than we are in the things that are visible.

The only safe way to decide which direction to go is by learning to distinguish between the voices we hear. There are always three sources of voices: there's God's voice, our own voice, and the devil's voice. We must learn to distinguish among these three.

We must choose to eliminate all foggy areas in our lives. This is the key to being able to see and think clearly. Fog is very dangerous to drive into, especially a spiritual fog.

We believers should choose to build on what we hear on the inside, not what we see on the outside. There's a big difference between having an ability to do something, and being called and anointed to do it. As you have sat in church, you may have seen someone who has an ability to sing, but that is not necessarily evidence that the person has been called of God to the life of a singer. A gift is not a call.

I am not suggesting that when we have the ability to do something that God isn't directing us to use that ability. But ability should not be the only criterion for deciding whether or not we make a particular choice. Not only does the Lord give us a road map, He also provides direction signals, information signs, a vehicle, fuel, and time to get to our destination.

We need to be sensitive to what lies in the unseen. Many people have walked right over rich pools of oil or veins of gold, not realizing what lay just beneath their feet. Their vision was too limited. They only saw the ground, not the treasure hidden in it.

Look beyond what you see with your natural eyes. Listen with your spiritual ears. Keep your antenna up for God's perfect direction in your life.

IT IS MORE VALUABLE TO SEEK GOD'S PRESENCE THAN TO SEEK HIS PRESENTS.

The Bible presents four benefits of seeking God's presence.

The first benefit is joy. In Psalm 16:11 (NIV), the psalmist says of the Lord, *You have made known to me that path of life; you will fill me with joy in your presence, with eternal pleasures at your right hand.* We cannot help but experience great joy in our lives when we are in the presence of the Lord.

A second benefit of seeking God's presence is that it provides great light. In Psalm 89:15 (NIV) we read, *Blessed are those who have learned to acclaim you, who walk in the light of your presence, O Lord.* Wherever God is, there is great illumination. If there is a dark area in your life, an area in which you are having difficulty seeing, invite the presence of the Lord into that area. If you are having problems with your work, invite the presence of God on the job with you. If you are having difficulty at home, invite the presence of the Lord into your home. The mere presence of God will bring illumination and cause all darkness to leave. It will shed great light on your path.

A third benefit of seeking His presence is God's divine protection. Psalm 31:20 (NIV) says, *In the shelter of your presence you hide them from the intrigues of men; in your dwelling you keep them safe from the strife of tongues.* Thank God for His divine protection and shelter in our lives. Everyone needs a hiding place, a place of safety and refuge. The presence of God provides a shelter to keep us from men and their vain words against us. If you're troubled by other people and by what they are saying, invite God's presence into those circumstances. If you work in a negative atmosphere, one in which what men are saying or doing is creating problems for you, invite the presence of God into that situation. He will be a shelter, a hiding place for you.

The fourth benefit of seeking God's presence is found in 1 John 3:19 (NIV): *This then is how we know that we belong to the truth, and how we set our hearts at rest in his presence.* There is great peace and great rest in the presence of God. Trouble, nervousness, anxiety, unrest, all these flee from the presence of the Lord.

Invite God's presence wherever you are. He will encamp around about you every minute and be with you in every situation of life. In His presence you will find great joy and light, divine protection, peace, and rest.

WHEN WISDOM REIGNS, IT POURS.

We should expect wisdom to be given to us. The Bible says in James 1:5, *If any of you lack wisdom, let him ask of God, that giveth to all men liberally, and upbraideth not; and it shall be given him.*

When you have heard God's voice, you have heard His wisdom. Thank God for His powerful wisdom. It forces a passage through the strongest barriers.

Wisdom is seeing everything from God's perspective. It is knowing when and how to use the knowledge that comes from the Lord. The old saying is true, "He who knows nothing, doubts nothing." But it is also true that he who knows has a solid basis for his belief.

Just think, we human beings have available to us the wisdom of the Creator of the universe. Yet **so few drink at the fountain of His wisdom; most just rinse out their mouths.** Many may try to live without the wisdom of the bread of life, but they will die in their efforts.

The world doesn't spend billions of dollars for wisdom. It spends billions in search of wisdom. Yet it is readily available to everyone who seeks its divine source.

There are ten steps to gaining godly wisdom:

1. Fear God (Ps. 111:10.)
2. Please God (Eccl. 2:26.)
3. Hear God (Prov. 2:6.)
4. Look to God (Prov. 3:13.)
5. Choose God's way (Prov. 8:10,11.)
6. Be humble before God (Prov. 11:2.)
7. Take God's advice (Prov. 13:10.)
8. Receive God's correction (Prov. 29:15.)
9. Pray to God (Eph. 1:17.)
10. Know the Son of God (1 Cor. 1:30.)

WE STAND TALLEST
WHEN WE ARE ON OUR KNEES.

The strongest action that you can take in any situation is to go to your knees and ask God for help. Whatever is worth worrying about is certainly worth praying about. Prayer unlocks God's treasure chest of great ideas.

I will share with you one of my favorite prayers. It is one word: *help.*

"Help, help, help!"

When we pray, we must be simultaneously willing to take the action that God directs in answer to our prayer.

There are four levels of prayer:

Level #1 is petition: "Father, I need...."

Level #2 is intercession: "God, help...."

Level #3 is praise and thanksgiving: "Thanks, Lord!"

Level #4 is conversation: "Good morning, Father."

In Philippians 4:6,7 (NIV) the Apostle Paul counsels us, *Do not be anxious about anything, but in everything, by prayer and petition, with thanksgiving, present your requests to God. And the peace of God, which transcends all understanding, will guard your hearts and your minds in Christ Jesus.* In Colossians 4:2 (NIV) he says, *Devote yourselves to prayer, being watchful and thankful.*

There are twelve benefits to prayer:
1. Prayer defeats the devil (Matt. 18:18)
2. Prayer saves the unbeliever (Acts 2:21)
3. Prayer edifies the believer (Jude 20)
4. Prayer sends laborers into the harvest (Matt. 9:38)
5. Prayer heals the sick (James 5:13-15)
6. Prayer overcomes the impossible (Matt. 21:22)
7. Prayer changes the natural (James 5:17,18)
8. Prayer brings the right things to pass (Matt. 7:7-11)
9. Prayer imparts wisdom (James 1:5)
10. Prayer brings peace (Phil. 4:5-7)
11. Prayer guards against temptation (Matt. 26:41)
12. Prayer reveals God's answers (Luke 11:9,10)

HEARING TELLS YOU THAT THE MUSIC IS PLAYING; LISTENING TELLS YOU WHAT THE SONG IS SAYING.

One of the least developed skills among us human beings is that of listening. There are really two different kinds of listening. There is the natural listening in interaction with other people, and there is spiritual listening to the voice of God.

It has been said, "Men are born with two ears, but only one tongue, which indicates that they were meant to listen twice as much as they talk." In natural communication, leaders always "monopolize the listening." **What we learn about another person will always result in a greater reward than what we tell him about ourselves.** We need to learn to listen and observe aggressively. We must try harder to truly listen, and not just to hear.

In regard to spiritual listening, Proverbs 8:34,35 (NIV) quotes wisdom who says:

Blessed is the man who listens to me, watching daily at my doors, waiting at my doorway.

For whoever finds me finds life and receives favor from the Lord.

There is great wisdom and favor to be gained by listening.

Proverbs 15:31 (NIV) says, *He who listens to a life-giving rebuke will be at home among the wise.* Listening allows us to maintain a teachable spirit. It increases our "teach-ability." Those who give us a life-giving rebuke can be a great blessing to us.

The Bible teaches that we are to be quick to listen and slow to speak. (James 1:19.) We must never listen passively, especially to God. If we resist hearing, a hardening can take place in our lives. Callousness can develop. In Luke 16:31 (NIV), Jesus said of a certain group of people, ". . .'If they do not listen to Moses and the Prophets, they will not be convinced even if someone rises from the dead.' " The more we resist listening to the voice of God, the more hardened and less fine-tuned our hearing becomes.

There are results of spiritual hearing, as we see in Luke 8:15 (NIV). This passage relates to the parable of the sower: ". . . the seed on good soil stands for those with a noble and good heart, who hear the word, retain it, and by persevering produce a crop." Harvest is associated not only with persevering and good seed in good soil, but also with those people who hear the Word of God and retain it.

Fine-tune your natural and spiritual ears to listen and learn.

GOD IS NOT YOUR PROBLEM; GOD IS ON YOUR SIDE.

Some time ago I was eating at a Mexican fast food restaurant. As I stood in line for service I noticed in front of me a very poor elderly lady who looked like a street person. When it came her turn, she ordered some water and one taco. As I sat in the booth right next to her, I couldn't help but observe and be moved with compassion toward her. Shortly after I had begun my meal I went over to her and asked if I could buy some more food for her lunch. She looked at me and angrily asked, "Who are you?"

"Just a guy who wants to help you," I responded. She ignored me. I finished my meal about the same time she did, and we both got up to leave. I felt led to give her some money. In the parking lot I approached her and offered her some cash. Her only response to me was, "Stop bothering me." Then, she stormed off.

Immediately, the Lord showed me that this is often the way many of us respond to Him. When He calls out to us, seeking to bless us, we act as though we don't even know Who He is. We respond to His offer of blessing by asking," Who are You? What do You want from me?" The Lord, being the gracious God He is, continues to try to bless us. Yet we react by saying, "Stop bothering me."

We walk off, just as this lady did, missing out on the rich blessings of the Lord.

It's not the absence of problems that gives us peace; it's God's presence with us in the problems. In Matthew 28:20, Jesus sent His disciples into all the world, ordering them to preach the Gospel to every creature: *Teaching them to observe all things whatsoever I have commanded you; and, lo, I am with you alway, even unto the end of the world.* In Romans 8:38,39 (NIV), the Apostle Paul writes, *For I am convinced that neither death nor life, neither angels nor demons, neither the present nor the future, nor any powers, neither height nor depth, nor anything else in all creation, will be able to separate us from the love of God that is in Christ Jesus our Lord.* In verse 31 he declares, *What, then, shall we say in response to this? If God is for us, who can be against us?* A paraphrase might be, "If God is for us, who cares who is against us?"

In Psalm 145:18 (NIV), we read, *The Lord is near to all who call on him, to all who call on him in truth.* James 4:8 (NIV) admonishes us, *Come near to God and he will come near to you.* In Acts 17:27 (NIV) Paul speaks: " 'For in him we live and move and have our being.' "

Thank God that we can, without hesitation and with full confidence, lean on His eternal faithfulness.

LEARN THE ALPHABET FOR SUCCESS.

A Action
B   Belief
C   Commitment
D   Direction
E   Enthusiasm
F   Faith
G   Goals
H   Happiness
I   Inspiration
J   Judgment
K   Knowledge
L   Love
M   Motivation
N   Nonconformity
O   Obedience
P   Persistence
Q   Quality
R   Righteousness
S   Steadfastness

T   Thankfulness

U   Uniqueness

V   Vision

W   Wisdom

X   (E)xcellence

Y   Yieldedness

Z   Zeal

THE MEASURE OF A MAN IS NOT WHAT HE DOES ON SUNDAY, BUT RATHER WHO HE IS MONDAY THROUGH SATURDAY.

You don't have to come out of the Spirit realm. The same closeness, strength, joy, and direction you experience on Sunday, God intends for you to walk in the rest of the week. The devil is waiting to ambush you as you leave church. He wants to bring to your mind thoughts of fear, doubt, unbelief, and destruction.

That's why we believers must guard our minds and hearts. As spiritual creatures, we walk by faith, not by sight. (2 Cor. 5:7.) We are commanded to live in the Spirit and not in the natural.

A person whose eyes, ears, and mind are directed toward the world finds it difficult to hear God speaking to him. The Lord wants to talk to you at work, at lunch, at play — everywhere you go. Some of my greatest revelations from God have come not in my prayer closet, but rather "out of the blue" in the midst of my normal, everyday life.

Our inner man is always willing, but our natural man resists. That's what Jesus meant when He said to His disciples, *Watch and pray, that ye enter not into temptation; the spirit indeed is willing, but the flesh is weak* (Matt. 26:41).

The advantage of living and walking in the Spirit is that it keeps us on the right path. In Galatians 5:16,17 (NIV) the Apostle Paul writes: *So I say, live by the Spirit, and you will not gratify the desire of the sinful nature. For the sinful nature desires what is contrary to the Spirit, and the Spirit what is contrary to the sinful nature. They are in conflict with each other, so that you do not do what you want. But if you are led by the Spirit, you are not under law.*

Thank God that our relationship with Him is not a "some-time affair," it's an "all-the-time union." In the words of the old hymn, "He leadeth me! O blessed thought!"

GOD WILL USE YOU
RIGHT WHERE YOU ARE TODAY.

$\mathbf{Y}$ou don't need to do anything else for God to begin to use you now. You don't have to read another paperback book, listen to another cassette tape, memorize another scripture, plant another seed gift, or repeat another creed or confession. You don't even need to attend another church service before God will begin to make use of you.

God uses willing vessels, not brimming vessels. Throughout the Bible, in order to fulfill His plans for the earth, God used many people from all walks of life. He used:

1. Matthew, a government employee, who became an apostle.
2. Gideon, a common laborer, who became a valiant leader of men.
3. Jacob, a deceiver, whose name became Israel.
4. Deborah, a housewife, who became a judge.
5. Moses, a stutterer, who became a deliverer.
6. Jeremiah, a child, who fearlessly spoke the Word of the Lord.
7. Aaron, a servant, who became God's spokesman.
8. Nicodemus, a Pharisee, who became a defender of the faith.
9. David, a shepherd boy, who became a king.

10. Hosea, a marital failure, who prophesied to save Israel.
11. Joseph, a prisoner, who became prime minister.
12. Esther, an orphan, who became a queen.
13. Elijah, a homely man, who became a mighty prophet.
14. Joshua, an assistant, who became a conqueror.
15. James and John, fishermen, who became close disciples of Christ and were known as "sons of thunder."
16. Abraham, a nomad, who became the father of many nations.
17. Peter, a businessman, who became the rock on which Christ built His Church.
18. Jacob, a refugee, who became the father of the twelve tribes of Israel.
19. John the Baptist, a vagabond, who became the forerunner of Jesus.
20. Mary, an unknown virgin, who gave birth to the Son of God.
21. Nehemiah, a cupbearer, who built the wall of Jerusalem.
22. Shadrach, Meshach, and Abednego, Hebrew exiles, who became great leaders of the nation of Babylon.
23. Hezekiah, a son of an idolatrous father, who became a king renowned for doing right in the sight of the Lord.
24. Isaiah, a man of unclean lips, who prophesied the birth of God's Messiah.
25. Paul, a persecutor, who became the greatest missionary in history and author of two-thirds of the New Testament.

All God needs to use you is all of you!

A FINAL WORD

Be the whole person God called you to be. Don't settle for anything less. Don't look back. Look forward and decide today to take steps toward His plan for your life.

And remember First Thessalonians 5:24: *Faithful is he that calleth you, who also will do it.*

Additional copies of
An Enemy Called Average
are available from your local bookstore,
or directly from:

Insight International
P. O. Box 54996
Tulsa, OK 74155

(Volume discounts available)

John Mason is the founder and president of Insight International, a ministry dedicated to bringing excellence and efficiency to Christian ministries and businesses. Several hundred businesses and ministries throughout the United States and abroad have benefitted from his counsel. John Mason's ministry exhorts believers to exercise all their gifts and talents while fulfilling God's whole plan for their lives. He is the author of several leadership manuals and tape series. He holds a Bachelor of Science degree in Business Administration from Oral Roberts University.

He also has the call and a powerful anointing to preach and minister to churches, men's and women's organizations and other Christian groups.

John was blessed to be raised in a Christian home in Fort Wayne, Indiana, by his parents Chet and Lorene Mason. He, his wife Linda and their four children Michelle, Greg, Mike, and David currently reside in Tulsa, Oklahoma.

John Mason welcomes the opportunity to minister to your church, in conferences, retreats, or in men's, women's, and youth groups.

Available from Insight International are the following inspiring videos:

"Momentum: How To Get it, How To Have It, How To Keep It."

"The Good Things About Bad Things."

"Don't Quit."

Also available is the following tape series:

"An Enemy Called Average"

Send all prayer requests and inquiries to:

John Mason
Insight International
P. O. Box 54996
Tulsa, OK 74155